FRANCE

A PICTURE BOOK TO REMEMBER HER BY

Designed by
DAVID GIBBON

Produced by
TED SMART

CRESCENT BOOKS
NEW YORK

When Caesar marched his legions into Gaul in 57 B.C., he found a country inhabited by a number of tribes, most of them Celtic. The conquest was completed by 51 B.C. and for the next five centuries the country that was to become France was ruled from Rome. During this period of Roman domination, the population acquired the culture and language of their occupiers. When the Roman Empire finally fell into decline, foreign tribes invaded Gaul and mingled with the original population. One of these tribes was the Franks, who were to give their name to the country. In the 8th century Charlemagne made the country the centre of an enormous empire, but it was divided up again amongst his successors.

The history of France, since the division of the Carolingian Empire in 843, is one of a nation racked by divisive and devastating wars; the Hundred Years War with England being a prime example. But the nation has also produced efficient and talented leaders who have held the nation together in times of adversity. The contribution of the nation to world culture cannot be valued too highly and the ideals of Liberty, Equality and Fraternity had their origins in the bloody events of the 1789 Revolution; ideals that were to lead to the eventual overthrow of absolutism and feudalism throughout Europe.

The old province of Normandy belongs to the Northern part of the country and is known as 'the dairy of France' for its production of butter and cheese, not least the creamy Camembert. Its world-renowned products are an important source of income for its inhabitants and are not restricted to dairy produce. The numerous apple orchards provide fruit for cider, sparkling apple wine and Calvados, a strong apple brandy which is only distilled here. Amongst the small and large towns of Normandy, Rouen is perhaps the most famous. The crowning glory of the cathedral here is the beautiful *Tour de Beurre*; literally, the tower of butter. It was in front of this cathedral that Joan of Arc, France's patron saint, was burnt as a heretic in 1431.

The most famous landmark in Paris, the Eiffel Tower, stands silhouetted (facing page) against the evening sky.

To the west of Normandy lies Brittany, a beautiful holiday area with important seafaring traditions. Boats leave regularly from the numerous fishing harbours along the extensive, rugged coast to catch sardines, mackerel and lobsters.

Nerve centre and capital city of the country, Paris lies in the North of France beautifully situatd on both banks of the Seine. High above the city rises the Basilica of the Sacré-Coeur which, with its white domes and towers, is one of the many buildings which give the city its distinctive character. Others are the Opéra; the Louvre, which contains one of the richest art collections in the world; the enormous Gothic cathedral of Notre Dame and the Eiffel Tower, symbol of Paris.

The countryside around the capital is picturesque and, moreover, extremely fertile so that agriculture is the chief industry. A few kilometres south of Paris, in one of the most beautiful woodland areas of France, lies Fontainebleau with its famous château, the oldest part of which dates from the 10th century.

The Champagne region, east of Paris, is one of the flattest areas of the country. It has given its name to the most exquisite sparkling wine in the world. It requires a great deal of skill and hard work to produce first-class Champagne. The selected grape juice is stored in gigantic vessels or tanks until it can be bottled. Unlike many other wines, fermentation is not completed until after champagne has been bottled, which accounts for the sparkling effect. Another famous wine-growing area is Alsace-Lorraine, where hops also flourish. Wine and beer are therefore – apart from the exquisite Strasbourg goose-liver pâté – the most famous products of this area. For centuries, this border area on the Rhine between Germany and France was disputed and changed ownership several times. Today – now that Europe is growing closer together – these differences have been relegated to the past.

One of the most beautiful parts of France is Burgundy, also a major wine-growing area. Montrachet, Chablis, Mâcon and Beaujolais are names well-known to every connoisseur; the wines come from the sunny slopes of the Côte d'Or. Gastronomically, too, Burgundy has much to offer, including dishes like boeuf à la bourguignonne, vineyard snails and the sharp Dijon mustard.

The excellent Provencal cuisine is given a special flavour by the addition of olive oil, garlic and aromatic herbs. The Côte d'Azur, or Riviera, with its fashionable seaside resorts of Nice, Cannes and St Tropez, is probably the best-known region of Provence. The extensive, sandy beaches, the calm, blue Mediterranean and a wonderful climate have an irresistible attraction for both French and foreign visitors. The neighbouring Camargue forms a stark contrast – a wild, sinister marshland area on the Rhône delta. Here, there are half-wild horses and black bulls, which are bred for the bullfighting arenas of Southern France.

The Southwest is one of the most interesting areas of the country. The main city, Bordeaux, is surrounded by vineyards which produce, among other wines, the top-quality St Emilion and Sauternes in addition to Cognac and Armagnac, the most prized brandies in the world. The delightful countryside gives ever-changing impressions: the silvery beaches and sand dunes of Les Landes, the miles of fragrant pine forests and the Dordogne Valley, which is famous for its caves with their prehistoric wall paintings.

Rich, superb truffles are the speciality of Périgord. They grow under the earth near oak trees, and young pigs are used to sniff them out. As soon as the pig has found a truffle, it is given some corn as a reward, and to prevent it eating the precious find. This is a good example of the care the French take to ensure that their cuisine remains an art. Here, more

---

Small fishing boats (top left) lie moored in the calm waters off the coast of Brittany. In the background is the attractive, enclosed town of Concarneau.

The town of Brest (bottom left), an important naval base and commercial port, lies at the western extremity of Brittany.

Virtually all Brittany's history and legends are intimately associated with the sea. The Côte Sauvage (facing page), part of the long, thin peninsula of Quiberon, is noted for its rugged grandeur.

than anywhere else, eating is considered to be one of the great pleasures in life, and excellent wines complement every meal. Travelling through the different areas of the country, with their examples of wonderful architecture, the varied, unspoilt countryside and the enjoyment of the different specialities provides a rare and perfect pleasure, not to be missed.

Voltaire maintained : "Paris is an enormous city full of idle people, who have an opinion on everything and think they know everything, who talk and listen a great deal, but who see little". And Emerson said quite rightly: "The difference between London and Paris is that Paris is there for foreigners and London is there for the English".

The Provencal troubadours were well-established leaders of French culture by early medieval times. The ensuing literary period is characterised by tales of knight errantry, such as the *Chanson de Roland. The Romance of the Rose* and the biography of King Louis IX are examples of morality prose. The great poet of the late Middle Ages was Villon, who mixed serious, comic and dramatic elements in his poetry. In the 16th century, there was a revival of learning and of interest in the Classical period. The most remarkable results of the

The ruins of the Château de Guitlard dominate the splendid landscape (top left) at Les Andelys in Normandy. The château was built in the 12th century by Richard the Lionheart, King of England.

The impressive memorial (top right) commemorates one of the Allied landings in Normandy during the Second World War.

Lakes and rivers, hills and woods, lush fields and fertile gardens characterise the splendid landscape of Normandy (bottom left).

(Bottom right): on the south side of the mouth of the Seine, opposite Le Havre, lies the small but important port of Honfleur.

In the Basque country, near the Spanish border, is situated the fishing and seaside resort of Saint Jean-de-Luz (overleaf).

Beautiful beaches, like those (top left) near the pretty little town of Dinan, are typical of those to be found on the north coast.

At the mouth of the Rance is the seaside resort of St Servan (below). From here it is not far to one of the favourite holiday resorts of Brittany, St Malo.

Perched on the top of a mass of granite is the stately church of St Michel (facing page), dating from the 11th and 12th centuries. The monastery buildings on the north side date from the 13th century and many of the fortifications were added later. Mont St Michel was used as a prison by Napoleon I and, over the years, saw the arrival and departure of 12,000 prisoners, until its closure in 1863 on the orders of Napoleon III.

movement are found in lyric poetry, and especially in the poetry of the *La Oléiade* group and their outstanding representative Ronsard; in the works of the great Renaissance thinker, atheist and sceptic Michel de Montaigne, author of *Les Essais*; in the *Heptameron* by Marguerite d'Angoulême and in Rabelais' extraordinary work *Gargantua and Pantagruel*. The last is considered to be one of the most important creations in world literature, full of riotous mirth, wit and wisdom, sometimes lewd or even obscene, and always with the motto: "Do what you will".

In The 17th century reason, moderation and clarity of the intellect became important virtues in France as elsewhere. These were given their clearest philosophical expression in the *Traitement de la Méthode* by Descartes, where these virtues are exemplified. Descartes' work is the first of a long series of no less inspired books, like Pascal's *Pensées*, where reason and clarity are connected with sensitivity, mysticism and the fear of life and death. The most important representatives of the poetry of this century are the elegant Malherbe and the poet and fabulist, La Fontaine. This was also the great period of the French Classical theatre, with personalities like Corneille, the author of *Le Cid* and other plays, which manifest the influence of the Spanish theatre; Racine, whose strictly formal plays like *Britannicus* stand out for their large-scale structure, and finally that inspired writer of comedies: Molière. Other writers, too, should be mentioned; like Perrault with his stories, La Rochefoucauld, author of the *Maximes* and Boileau, La Bruyère, Madame de La Fayette, Lesage, Bossuet and Fénelon.

Holidaymakers sun themselves on the white sands of Beg-Meil in Brittany (top left).
The towers of the cathedral of Quimper (bottom left), in Brittany, seen from the canal.
Hoping for a good catch, a fisherman in the port of Beg-Meil gets his boat ready to sail (facing page).

The 18th century was dominated politically and culturally by an expansionist France. It was as a result of the consolidation of power and reason that the century was called the "Age of Reason". Amongst the thinkers we find the characteristic representatives of this period headed by Montesquieu and "*Les*

Paris, probably the most romantic capital in the world, is particularly fascinating at night (facing page). The majestic Sacré-Coeur, its white dome floodlit against the velvet sky, is a compelling tourist attraction, whilst the outdoor cafés in Montmartre offer refreshment and a chance to sit and rest between rounds of sight-seeing.

Notre Dame Cathedral (top right and below), sited on the 'Ile de la Cité, in the Seine, was the coronation place of countless kings and emperors for centuries past.

Encyclopédistes" with Voltaire, Diderot and D'Alembert, whom Jean Jacques Rousseau is supposed to have followed. Rousseau takes up once again the tradition of feeling, which despite the triumph of reason was not entirely lost, and with his *Emile* and *Les Confessions* paved the way for the Romantics. Other writers who should not be left out are the dramatist Marivaux, and the novelists Bernardin de Saint-Pierre and l'Abbé Prévost. The Revolutionary period at the end of the 18th century was one of great talkers and complex erotic works, exemplified by the books of the Marquis de Sade and of Choderlos de Laclos.

The Romantic era broke with the French tradition of reason and replaced it with one of feeling, and an evocation of the Middle Ages. The movement started in the northern countries and then spread to France. Chateaubriand was the first major figure of the movement. Lamartine, Vigny and especially Victor Hugo, in their novels, plays and poems, show themselves as the most important creators of Romantic literature. Musset, Gautier and Dumas followed in their wake.

But before long a counter to Romanticism emerged: Realism. The

The Arc de Triomphe (top left), built by Napoleon to honour his victorious army, has become a symbol of France. Leading to this great monument is the fashionable Champs-Elysées, one of the foremost shopping streets in the world. Montmartre, in its heyday frequented by artists such as Henri de Toulouse-Lautrec, is famous for the 'Moulin Rouge' (bottom left). Sadly, many of the area's attractions have now either closed, or been converted into cinemas. The Louvre Museum, (top and bottom right) opened in 1793, probably established the blueprint of what all museums should be like. Work on this building was started as early as 1204 under King Philippe Auguste and completed during the reign of Louis XIV. Some of the most famous works of art in the world are exhibited here, including Leonardo da Vinci's 'Mona Lisa'.

most important representatives of this movement are Balzac, with his great series of novels *La Comédie Humaine*; Flaubert who, with his *Madame Bovary*, went beyond this new style to some extent; Stendhal, whose *Le Rouge et Le Noir* laid the foundations stone for the modern novel; and Daudet, Fromentin and the Goncourt brothers. At the end of the century, Realism passed into Naturalism with such authors as Zola, Maupassant and Huysmans.

In the 20th century we encounter a series of contrasting trends. On the one hand we find the tormented scepticism of Loti, the humanism of Anatole France and the nationalism of Barrès, and on the other the rebellion against traditional values of the dramatist Jarry or the versatile Jean Cocteau. The poets of the new generation for their part follow the great examples of the 19th century: Baudelaire, Verlaine, Lautréamont. A list of the great writers of this century would be very long indeed. We come across the names of

From the top of the Eiffel Tower may be seen the breath-taking panorama (above); one of the most spectacular views in all Paris.

Across the elegant Pont Alexandre III is seen the Promenade des Invalides (bottom left). L'Hôtel des Invalides was founded in 1671 by Louis XIV as a hospital for seriously wounded soldiers, and is still used for this purpose today. In addition to Napoleon's tomb, it also houses an impressive collection of weapons and armour.

Above the Moulin Rouge (bottom right) rises the 120-metre-high hill of Montmartre, which overlooks the whole city and in the past was, from a military point of view, the key to Paris. In the background rises the glorious white Basilica of the Sacré-Coeur with its unmistakeable bell tower and cupolas.

philosophers like Bergson, Sartre, Merleau-Ponty, Marcel and Althusser; novelists like Proust, who wrote the great *A la Recherche du Temps Perdu*, Gide, Bernanos, Céline, Camus, Becket, and poets such as Paul Valéry, Paul Eluard, Paul Claudel or Saint-John Perse.

The fine arts also constitute an important cultural legacy from the nation's past – an inheritance that includes architecture, sculpture, painting and the magnificent stained-glass windows of the cathedrals. The best architectural examples are the cathedrals of Tours, Angoulême, Chartres, Amiens and Laôn; the abbeys of Tournus, Cluny and Charlieu and palaces like those of Avignon, Poitiers and the Thermes de Julien. The Renaissance, which originated in Lombardy, was adopted at the court of Francois I, but it soon deteriorated into Mannerism, the most interesting representative of which was the painter Cousin. Important figures of the Baroque art style are the painters Lorrain and Poussin.

Behind the Pont au Change (top left), stands the impressive building of the Palais de Justice, which covers the whole width of the Ile de la Cité. It contains the Conciergerie, one of the most famous prisons in the world, where Marie Antoinette, Danton, Robespierre and many others spent their last days.

Enclosed within the walls of the palace stands the beautiful old Sainte Chapelle (centre left), with over a thousand biblical scenes adorning its windows. The building counts as one of the most important art treasures in the city.

Les Invalides (bottom left) illuminated at twilight, with a cannon in the foreground.

With the Eiffel Tower in the background, the twenty fountains of the Palais de Chaillot create a magical atmosphere (facing page). The Tower was constructed by the eminent engineer Alexandre Eiffel on the occasion of the International Exhibition in 1889. When it was originally built it was considered that it would have a life-span of no more than twenty years.

The outstanding figures of the age of Classicism, under the patronage of the Bourbons, were eminent architects like Le Vau; Perrault, (who built the colonnades of the Louvre); Hardouin-Mansart, (the architect of the Palace of Versailles); the great landscape designer Le Notre and F. Mansart. The painting of this era is best represented by the works of Mignard, Rigaud, Le Moine, Van Loo and La Tour. Another great era of French art was the Rococo period.

It is the painters of the 19th and 20th centuries, however, who have contributed most to France's artistic fame; first of all David and Ingres, but especially towards the middle and end of the last century, Corot, Millet and Daubigny, who interpreted nature in an original way and paved the way for Impressionism.

Manet was the first great Impressionist, followed by Monet, Renoir, Pissarro, Sisley, Degas and Seurat who, together with other painters such as Fantin-Latour, De Chavannes, Cézanne, Gauguin, Toulouse-Lautrec and Bonnard, steered painting in the Western world in a new direction and made art extremely popular. These artists carried out almost scientific

The majestic Basilica of the Sacré-Coeur is shown (facing page) with its marvellous terraces and its flights of steps.

Pavement cafés are a feature of the Champs Elysées (top right), seen with the familiar Arc de Triomphe in the background.

It was on the Place de la Concorde (centre right), that Louis XVI and Marie Antoinette were publicly guillotined. Beyond the fountain stands an obelisk, a gift from Egypt, which was sent to Paris to replace the memorial to Louis XV, destroyed during the Revolution.

One of the most richly adorned buildings in Paris is the Opéra (bottom right), the largest opera house in the world. The stairs and ceiling of white marble are decorated with paintings by Chagall, and attract many tourists.

(Overleaf) can be seen the glorious Palace and gardens of Versailles.

Azay-le-Rideau (top right), with its grey-blue roof and massive, white stone walls, is partly built on supports in the River Indre, a tributary of the Loire.

The Château de Luynes (facing page), dating from the 15th and 16th centuries, is one of the numerous châteaux of the Loire. This wonderful building is now a luxury hotel, where guests can enjoy genuine antiques and a lovely, wooded setting.

A wide and deep moat surrounds the Château at Sully-sur-Loire (below) with its huge towers. Here, Henri IV's finance minister lived after the king's assassination until he, too, was murdered.

Set in the middle of a park as large as Paris is the Château de Chambord (overleaf), once the favourite château of King Francois I.

research into the art of painting, and the painters of the 20th century followed them along this road.

The Impressionists introduced themselves to the public as a group in 1874. The main thing they had in common was their down-to-earth attitude to the world. It was their belief that artists in search of subjects should not look to history, religion, mythology or literature. They should, instead, find their subjects in the world as it existed around them; in the streets, in the country, at railway stations, at fêtes, at horse-races; anywhere where there was light and colour.

Such an attitude seemed like blasphemy to everyone, public and critics alike. It was as if the Impressionists painted with their feet instead of with their hands. Nevertheless, they made people aware of the beauty of ordinary things, unrelated to fame or history. Gradually they evolved a doctrine and a technique. The English art critic Clive Bell wrote about this subject as follows: 'If only people would look at what was really there instead of pretending to see the labels imposed on things by the practical intellect or, worse still, by pretentious drawing-masters, they would discover that everything in the garden, or the street, or anywhere else is lovely – and presumably would buy impressionist pictures'. Although the term 'Impressionism' is not quite correct, it is yet expressive in that it points out that our eyes receive the sensations caused by light. The Impressionist painter records his visual impressions faithfully

Chenonceau (facing page and bottom right) is a magnificent château in the valley of the Loire, and was the favourite residence of Catherine de Medici.

The Château de Saumur (top right) is sited on a hill above the confluence of the Thouet and Loire.

Not far from Tours lies the Château d'Amboise (centre right), with its mixture of Gothic and Renaissance styles. Nearby is the house where Leonardo da Vinci lived and where, legend has it, he died in the arms of King Francois I.

and modestly. He observes 'that colour merges into colour; that bounding lines, like perspective, are intellectual makeshifts and that shadows are neither black nor brown but full of a variety of colours. Thus the Impressionists use pure colours, which they apply with

---

The formal, beautiful gardens of the 16th-century Château de Villandry are featured on these pages. The lush greenery of the box hedges and the colourful, stylised floral arrangements are seen at their best in the summer sunshine.

Contrasting with the peace and tranquillity of the Loire Valley is the rooftop view (overleaf) of Strasbourg, one of the largest cities in France. This aerial view shows the picturesque old town. In the background stand modern, high-rise buildings.

short brush strokes in the form of dots or dashes.'

It is evident that the original style, which was followed faithfully for the first ten years of Impressionism, from 1872 to 1882, was merely a starting point. Then every painter went his own way, the strong personality of each of them overcoming their spiritual affinity and common artistic origins. In the eyes of some critics Degas was never an Impressionist and Renoir was barely one. At all events, it was Cézanne who developed the movement and left the most influential work for others to follow. Like literature, 20th century fine art in France was characterised by an interest in experimentation, with the first four decades of the century governed by the radical *Avante-garde* movement.

At the beginning there was modernism in architecture, in the shape of furniture and glass objects and in arts and crafts. The use of reinforced concrete enabled Le Corbusier (who was in fact Swiss) to revolutionise architecture. The sculptor Maillol, on the other hand, chose the classical path. In painting, the 'Fauves' asserted themselves with their exaltation of colours, which were intended to release strong emotions in the observer, typical examples being the works of Marquet, Derrain, Dufy and especially Matisse.

It was also at the beginning of this century that Braque and Picasso

Bonnieux (top left) is one of a number of fortified, hill-top villages near Avignon, in Provence.

The Palace of the Popes in Avignon (top right) was used from 1309 to 1377 as the Papal residence.

Cattle graze peacefully on the slopes below the beautiful Château de Berzel in Burgundy (bottom right).

The tiny village of Bonneval, over 3,300 feet above sea level, high in the French Alps (bottom left), is transformed in winter into a lovely ski resort, one of many in the region.

The golden leaves of the vines give the Berz de la Ville area a dream-like aspect (overleaf).

together 'discovered' Cubism. This style constructs a painting using several levels, and assumes that objects can be seen not only from one side but from several sides simultaneously. Other painters who followed this path were Metzinger, Marcoussis, Gris, Villon and Fresnaye. Some sculptors, like R. Duchamp-Villon, produced Cubist sculptures. Amongst the Orphists, Delauney stands out, and amongst the Surrealists, Tunguy and Dubuffet (as well as several Spanish artists, like Dali and Miró, who are closely connected with the life and art of France). Of the Informalists, Masson, Bazaine and Fautrier should be mentioned.

Music developed in a similar way to the visual arts and reached peaks during the Romantic and Gothic periods. In the 14th century, Guillaume de Machaud in particular stands out; in the following centuries, however, the protagonists were foreign musicians (Italian and German) who settled in France. The greatest composer of the 18th century was Couperin. In the 19th century Auber, Berlioz, Gounod, Massenet, Délibes, Lalo, Saint-Seans, Vincent d'Indy, Dukas, Charpentier and Chabrier are among the best-known. The most famous composers of our century are Debussy, Ravel, Honegger, Milhaud, Messiaen and Boulez.

From the earliest days of the cinema, France produced important actors and directors; a tradition which began towards the end of the 19th century with the Lumière brothers. One of the first to stand out was Méliès, who used amazing trick photography in his films *The Journey*

Food and wine play an important part in French life, and in a market in Quimper (facing page) shoppers wait to buy, from a white-coiffed Breton fish seller, succulent shellfish, a speciality of Brittany.

Bordeaux (this page), one of the large wine-growing areas, is famed for such wines as Château Lafite, Latour and Margaux, and for the renowned brandies from Cognac and Armagnac, highly valued by connoisseurs throughout the world.

to the Moon and *The Conquest of the Pole.*
One of the earliest film companies was
the well-known Pathé, under the
direction of F. Zecca. Soon further
companies appeared, like the Gaumont
company with its director Feuillade, or
Eclair, run by Jaset, who brought the
Nick Carter series to life. Before the
outbreak of the First World War, the
French tried their hand at the artistic
cinema, working with well-known
artists.

The war proved a temporary setback for
the film industry. Then producers like
Abel Gance, Jean Epstein and
Germaine Dulac came forward. The
Surrealists, like Cocteau, used the film
as a medium of expression, although it
was the Spaniard, Buñuel, who created
the most convincing films of this genre in
France. An outstanding producer was
René Clair with films like *Sous les toits de
Paris.* Marcel Carné's film *Quai des
Brumes,* made in 1938, should not be
overlooked either. But perhaps the most
famous producer of all was Jean Renoir
(the son of the painter), who made the
films *La Grande Illusion* (the subject of
which was the First World War) and *La
Règle du Jeu.* René Clement, Clouzet,
Jacques Becker and the humorist
Jacques Tati (*Mon Oncle*) are names that
became famous after the Second World
War.

The films of Robert Bresson are
impressive for their austerity. Later the
films of the 'Nouvelle Vague' produced a
considerable change; their main

Grenoble (top left), the capital of the
Dauphiné, has a splendid 12th century
cathedral and the famous monastery,
La Chartreuse, where, using secret old
recipes, the green and gold-yellow
Chartreuse liqueur is distilled.

Long, straight, tree-lined avenues are
very much a feature of the towns and
cities (bottom left) of this part of France.
Clinging to the hillside above a
tributary of the River Rhône is the small
town of Crest (top right).

Valence (bottom right) was established
before the Roman occupation and has a
picturesque Romanesque cathedral
dating from the year 1095.

representatives being Jean-Luc Godard, Francois Truffaut, Claude Chabrol, Eric Rohmer, Jacques Démy, Agnès Varda, Louis Malle and Alain Resnais, who became famous through his research work in the field of cinematic mediums of expression.

It has been said that in Germany and Italy, it was the nation that first came into existence and then the State evolved. In France, however, the State came first and only then the nation. However it evolved, the French State is a model of centralism and has an ability to withstand radical change. Here, the impersonal state always lasts longer than personalised society. Centralism is where the king or president is, as with Paris, and this centralism has applied almost throughout the entire history of the country.

The official language of the country is French, even though other languages are also spoken, for instance Occetan in the Languedoc or Catalan in Roussillon. German is spoken in large parts of Alsace, Flemish on the North Sea coast, Breton in Brittany, Basque in the French Basque country and Italian in Corsica.

French, like English and Spanish, is a world language and was traditionally regarded as the language of culture: it was thought that English was better for

Annecy (top left), a delightful town at the northern end of Lake Annecy, is the capital of the Haute-Savoie region. Worthy of especial note are the old castle and palace, whilst in the oldest part of the town arcaded lanes, alternating with canals, are reminiscent of Venice.

(Bottom left): a sparkling fountain in Toulouse.

The wild and rugged landscape of the national park of Vanoise, with its mountain stream cascading down the rocks (top right), is sharply contrasted with the idyllic scene (bottom right) on the Isère, near Grenoble.

White, frothy clouds surround the snow-covered peaks of the Pelvoux-Massif, which tower majestically over the sparsely inhabited and thickly-wooded valleys (overleaf).

trade, but for more lofty subjects, the French language was considered more suitable.

From an economic point of view, France is one of the most highly developed countries in the world, and the reason for this is the attention the country has always paid to scientific endeavour and the ideal of expediency, combined with the strength of the people and their enterprising spirit.

France's national income is the sixth largest in the world, and its population has the seventh largest per capita income. The country has been extensively industrialised and its trade stands on firm foundations. The working population consists of 70% men and 30% women, but the proportion of working women is rising. France also has many foreign workers, especially from North Africa, Spain and Italy.

The most densely populated areas of the country are Paris and its suburbs, the Lyons area, the North-west, Lorraine and the Marseilles area. Since the end of the Second World War, the State has taken a direct role in economic planning with the nationalisation of railways, air and shipping companies etc. Forward-looking, 5-year development plans have been advances, as in the Soviet Union, with the difference, however, that in France only indirect control is exercised. Agricultural development, on the other hand, has progressed in a very irregular fashion. The high yields from the large, mechanised farms in the Paris area contrast with the smaller yields in other parts of the country, where excessive division of properties and antiquated equipment and methods cause many

One of the most popular winter sport resorts is Lac de Tignes in the Savoie region. The snow-covered slopes, which are excellent for skiing, are reflected in the still waters of the lake (top and bottom left), while the shores of the lake (centre left) are also suitable for other sports activities.

Val d'Isère nestles in the mountains (facing page) and is connected with the skiing resort of Lac de Tignes by an extensive lift and funicular system.

problems. This has led to an increasing population drift from the countryside to the towns.

Because of its world-wide reputation, French wine deserves special mention. Wine production is about sixty million hectolitres annually and there are large surpluses. The best-known wine-growing areas are Alsace, Bordeaux, Burgundy, the Loire valley, the Rhône valley and, for sparkling wine, Champagne. The production of Cognac and other brandies is also considerable. The country has extensive coal mining areas in the North and in Lorraine, but only limited resources of oil so that it is largely dependent on imports from the Middle East. The valuable iron ore deposits in Lorraine are among the most important in the world.

Apart from some large industrial conglomerates, most businesses in France are of moderate size. For obvious reasons, the most industrially-developed parts of the country are those with the highest density of population. There are some very large companies in the iron and steel, chemical, aluminium and automobile industries, Renault, Citroën and Peugeot for example, and also other companies which are particularly export-orientated. The aerospace industry has had a noticeable upturn in recent years, especially with military aircraft such as the Mirage and Mystère.

In 1947, France signed the Geneva Agreement (GATT) in economic cooperation. In 1948 it was among the founder states of the Organisation for European Economic Cooperation

Near the Italian border lies Menton (top left), sheltered by the slopes of the Alpes Maritimes.

The pretty resort of Villefranche (centre left), on the French Riviera, is almost a suburb of Nice. Yachts of all kinds seek shelter in its splendid bay (top right).

Corsica (bottom left), a charming, unspoiled island with its wild country-side, its delightful coastal villages and solid towns, is sharply contrasted with the fashionable Côte d'Azur (bottom right).

(OEEC), and in 1951 it joined the European Coal and Steel Community, the foundation stone of the EEC, which came into existence in 1957.

The French have always been concerned with the difference between well-mannered and impertinent people. The French have frequently theorised about this phenomenon themselves. Manners – *Politesse* – is a tradition which stretches back to the elegant days of the Bourbon Court. But impertinence and lack of control also have their role to play as is shown by the unexpected outbreaks in everyday, social and political life.

The French have always insisted on very strict rules of behaviour. Good, formal education pervades every level of society. The most interesting fact is that French politeness is encouraged as much by reason as by experience. People are polite, because they wish to live well; the principle of reason applied to good living.

It is not surprising, however, that such formal behaviour is often mixed with the exact opposite. France is a country which is just as revolutionary as it is polite. While a large part of society conforms, Villon or Rabelais introduced coarse notes to create a reaction. The admonishment 'Behave yourself' is countered by Rabelais, with 'Do what you will'. Overly-refined behaviour found its antithesis in the French Revolution. The cultured *savoir vivre* contrasts with the demands of the rebellious students in May 1968 for 'Free expression to power!' The dramatist, Jarry, became the centre of a tremendous scandal when he allowed an

Cannes, one of today's most popular Riviera resorts, was a small fishing port until 1834. In the harbour (top left) the little fishing boats are almost lost amongst the host of anchored yachts. Luxurious hotels, offices and apartments line the wide beach promenade (bottom left).

A view of the sun-drenched town of Nice, with the famous Promenade des Anglais, is shown (top right). The hotels and amusement areas of the town are world renowned (below right).

actor to tell a dirty joke. In England exaggerated formality is countered by witty and paradoxical humour, while France is often preoccupied with coarseness.

But politeness and argumentativeness, according to the French themselves, do not divide the country into the good and the bad; instead the two facets simply exist side by side in each individual. Even a well educated person always has a fund of what Rabelais or the Marionette Theatre raised to artistic heights. In France, people try to be both distinguished and vulgar, noble and democratic.

No less interesting is the fact that French politeness represents an attempt to achieve naturalness, in a round-about way, through artificiality. This differs very distinctly from the formal politeness which is characteristic of other European countries, except for those like Austria or Poland, which have copied the French model.

To be natural, in most other countries, means to act according to one's feelings, but in France it is something that requires in-depth study and is dominated by reason. The fact that the philosopher Descartes raised mere common sense to an all-embracing level is well-known. This 'common sense' is not a result of human nature, but is a deliberate effect achieved by reason and the search for balance.

Another deep-rooted characteristic of the French is *l'esprit*, which cannot be easily translated as 'spirit'. *Esprit* is something light, which, like 'la politesse', helps to make life more

St Tropez (top left and top right) has a great attraction for famous, and not so famous, artists.

Along the coast from Cannes are the other well-known resorts of St Raphael, St Maxine and St Tropez. Palm trees, splendid bays and clean water make St Raphael an ideal holiday resort (bottom left).

(Below right): many of the yachts and villas of St Tropez and St Maxime belong to the rich and the famous who seek refuge in the South of France.

agreeable. As was mentioned earlier, France is situated between the countries of the European North and South, not only geographically but culturally as well. The German attitude to life is that man, tortured by self-doubts, reaches his goal after long thought – like the architect looking for a rock on which the foundations of his building will be firmly based. The Italian, on the other hand, believes more in life and spontaneity, while the French maintain their 'esprit' and combine both concepts – man should think in order to live well. Moderation and tolerance are essentially French virtues.

Love, too, is a typically French subject. It was the French who first categorised those two great aspects of love, which exist throughout Europe: romantic or elevated, and physical or base. The former was immortalised by the Provencal troubadours of the Southern courts, whose tales consisted, to a large extent, of spiritualizing the erotic instincts. Because adultery was strictly forbidden, love changed to something purely platonic and spiritual – at least in theory.

In the 18th century, the bored aristocracy deteriorated to the other, purely physical, love. One aristocrat once said: "in order to love properly, the most important thing is not to fall in love". He argued that if you do, problems immediately arise; jealousy,

---

On a particularly quiet part of the coast lies Cavalaire, with its shimmering blue waters sparkling in the sun (top left).

Cassis (centre left), lying twelve miles east of Marseilles, is noted for its great scenic beauty.

Originally called Cithérista, La Ciotat (bottom left) has been an important naval centre since the 16th century.

The enchanting bay of Le Lavandou (top right) offers the visitor, in addition to its fishing harbour, marvellous views of some of the smaller islands of the Mediterranean.

The beautiful Ile de Port Cros (bottom right), with its lush green backdrop of trees, is one of the rocky Iles d'Hyères, situated just off the coast.

psychological claims of ownership and so on.

And just as a good wine goes with a French meal, so a third person goes with love. To prevent love becoming purely an instinctive matter, the presence of a third person is required, to give it spice, make it more of a challenge and therefore more interesting. This is the philosophical basis of adultery and the triangular relationship.

Such situations only work for those who know that it is a game, an art, and France has traditionally produced numerous experts in this field. In this sense, France has given the world more artists than any other country: artists in the art of living. The fact that French women pay considerable attention to their appearance, have fine manners and are good conversationalists, dress well, make up well and give the impression of a certain refinement, is proof that women fundamentally belong as much to society as men. Despite all the changes, the tradition continues. And it is a long tradition, for women have long played a leading role in French society. It was women who held literary, social and political salons in the 18th century and Madame de Pompadour gained great political influence as mistress of Louis XV.

Reflected in the shimmering water is the delightful fishing town of Martigues (top left), which is situated in the Besse Basin, near the large port of Marseilles. La Grande Motte (bottom left), with its futuristic hotel and apartment blocks which have been built close to the water's edge, is one of the newest resorts and is close to the town of Montpelier. Marseilles (facing page) is the most important port in France. It looks back on two and a half thousand years of history, to when the first Greek settlers arrived. There are several islands along the coast, including that on which stands the infamous Château d'If, from which the legendary Count of Montecristo is reputed to have made his spectacular escape.

French gastronomy does not concentrate so much on the stomach as on the art of courting the senses of smell and taste. That the end justifies the means is perfectly demonstrated here. It is like dressing, which is more an adornment than a means to cover nakedness. If you want to compare English, German and Spanish cuisines you do so on French criteria. French gastronomy does not need to be compared; it is unique.

The French word 'gourmet' describes a person with expert knowledge of exquisite dishes and wines. Only a Frenchman, the novelist Daudet, could write: "I am genuinely convinced that understanding between nations is only possible in the area of gastronomy". The statement is not quite true, because a Frenchman would be able to come to an understanding with an Englishman in France but the same could not necessarily be said about a Frenchman in England.

The typical cuisine of the country has, over the centuries, evolved into a combination of courtly, traditional and foreign arts of cooking. The great synthesis between these three cuisines occurred in the 19th century. French cooks, or chefs, gained such high reputations that they were exported abroad as if they were engineers. Some of them acquired real fame, like Béchamel, who invented the famous sauce which carries his name.

Carême, the great 19th century theoretician, wrote down the laws applying to this art, before he became chef to Rothschild. Curnonsky was raised to the rank of a prince in the year 1927 by 5,000 gourmets. In fact, his name was Saillant and like many other

Wild, snow-capped mountains; wooded, remote valleys with occasional isolated villages; grazing cattle on the slopes; all are typical of the Pyrenean scenery (facing page and bottom right). The lovely old medieval town of Estaing (above right), with its picturesque castle and bridge mirrored in the still waters, is a characteristic example of the rural beauty of this region of France.

chefs he refused tempting offers in order to devote himself entirely to his calling. Sanche de Gramont gives the following resumée of the French culinary art: "The main prerequisite for a good cuisine is the country itself, and France is in the happy position of not only producing everything it needs itself, but also producing excellent quality, like for example lamb pré salé, beef from Charollais, butter from Normandy, salmon from Adour, ducks from Nantes, truffles from Périgord and asparagus from the Loire area. The most widely varying ingredients are available in abundance. Little needs to be imported, though at present a large number of snails are imported from Eastern Europe and some goose liver from Israel. In France it has been possible to eat well since the Gauls settled as shepherds and acquired a taste for eating river fish prepared with vinegar and caraway and started raising their famous geese from Cambresis and discovered what a good taste there was to wild asparagus."

Lyons (top left) is, when industry, trade and population are taken into account, the third largest town in France after Paris and Marseilles.

In Orange there are several important ruins of Roman buildings. The well-known amphitheatre (bottom left) is an outstanding example.

Impressive even today are the medieval castle and walls of Carcassonne with their fifty-two well preserved towers (top and bottom right).

First published by Colour Library Books Ltd.
© Illustrations: Colour Library Books Ltd. Colour separations by La Cromolito, Milan, Italy.
Display and text filmsetting by Focus Photoset, London, England.
Printed and bound by JISA-RIEUSSET and EUROBINDER.
ISBN 0 517 25 0 195
CRESCENT 1984